TRUE PATH
Evolving

PAUL COLQUHOUN

First published in 2018 by Paul Colquhoun
Updated version published in 2020 by Paul Colquhoun
Email: followyourtruepath@gmail.com

Copyright © Paul Colquhoun 2018
ISBN: 9780648149156

Cover design by Jacqui Lynch, Preloaded Design
Design and layout by Paul Colquhoun

All rights reserved. No part of this publication may be reproduced, stored in, or introduced into a retrieval system, or transmitted in any form or by any means (electronic, mechanical, photocopying, recording or otherwise) without the prior written permission of the publisher.

A catalogue record for this book is available from the National Library of Australia

CONTENTS

FORWARD	5
INTRO	8
THE JOURNEY	19
THE BIGGER PICTURE	41
BODY	71
MIND	86
EGO	91
SOUL	101
SPIRIT	110
CONSCIOUS & SUBCONSCIOUS	125
LAW OF ATTRACTION	134
LET GO & LET BE	145
REFERENCES	154

FORWARD

Paul's book **True Path** shares a profound truth. For those who are beginning to awaken to something more, something deeper in their life, this book has your message!

I have personally worked closely with Paul for the past 12 months, and I have witnessed him embrace the principles in his life that he shares with his readers in this book. Paul has a heart that just wants to give… as he reaches new levels on his own journey, he wants to take others with him, and this book will do exactly that for all those who are ready.

Paul has written this book in a way that is

simple yet impacting. I believe the message of this book and the way it is delivered will reach the hearts of those who need it most.

If you allow it to, this book will be the beginning of an epic journey for you – a deep awakening that frees you from the limitations imposed on us all by a society who wants to keep us small, and take our power. This book will help you begin to find who you really are, and also, who you are not! Knowing that, you can claim your power back and live a life of purpose, the life that was meant for you!

My prayer for every reader is that this book births within you a desire to find out why you are here in this human experience, and what your mission is. The more of us that hunger to find this answer, the more we grow and rise to new levels of consciousness. The more we grow, the more value we can provide to others, and the more significant our lives become. Significance is fulfilling to the soul. May your life be blessed with that feeling every day, from this moment on.

As a special note, I wish to thank you Paul Colquhoun, for all that you are, and for all that you have grown through to be able to be here making this message available to others today. Congratulations for having the courage to print this book, and for making your voice heard, and your message felt!

Much love always, stay amazing!
Holly Nunan
Author, speaker, coach, radio show host
<u>www.thehollyeffect.com</u>
Feed your soul, settle your spirit and unbecome!

INTRO

First of all, thanks Holly Nunan for guiding me to this point and helping me decipher enough of my crap to allow me to start focusing on my true path. Thanks to the readers for being open enough to grab a copy. There's no coincidence you've got a copy in your hands like i found the book that changed my life, it just felt right to read. Not saying this is the book that will change your life but hopefully you'll find something.

Have you ever wondered why you're here, a coincidence, a lucky sperm, is it just evolution or are you the Golden Child...? No matter what your beliefs or religion you ended up being born here on Earth, now what...? Are you here to go study your ass off at school, to learn crap you'll hardly ever use,

…..damn…..how many times have you used a Bunsen Burner since you left school, …..not! Who's to say that the teacher's references are true or correct or even beneficial to humanity…..? Are you working a job you hate or simply bored, trading time for money just to pay the bills to barely survive, especially if you've got a house, a couple cars and family, then you're most likely under the pump, …..or are you staying in a relationship you're not enjoying, hanging out with people that you don't relate to anymore, ……look in the mirror and don't love what you see, …..always ill, ……why are others always so lucky or successful or happy and just never me, ……do i have a more worthy role on this planet just waiting for me…?, …..is it all worth the struggle, the worry, the stress, …..life can be bloody hard at times. I hate the saying, "Life wasn't meant to be easy"….yes it was, we've just made it hard, because no one has shown us any different, ……our crap got passed down to us through generations of mistakes and guessing, …..yes you can thank your parents and grandparents and teachers for the shit you're in, …..but they weren't to know, most decisions they've made were out of love while they were dealing with their shit, ...as you'll see in the upcoming chapters. Understandably, not everyone lives this way, and not all education or jobs are crap, we need education, industry, trades and professionals, but if you're reading this book then there's a good chance you're looking for some answers, a way out, the red pill, a bigger meaning to life, ...most of all peace, happiness, fulfillment and purpose, ...and that's why i'm writing, ...i can't wait, there's so many of you out there searching for some type of answer to make sense of it all, just as i was. Your true path, or soul journey, may involve education, industry, trades or be on a professional forum, a humanitarian journey, whatever, ...it depends on your background, nature and the way you've been groomed, ...so let's find out how to find your part in the bigger picture, enjoy this journey with me, ...and for those already aware, i hope you find that further seed of info or message to take you to the next level.

There's constant pressure in life to conform,

paying bills, getting out of bed when you'd just love to lay in, doing things that you really don't want to do just to pay bills, being the right partner/parent/mate, comparing yourself to others, and many other areas of life where the rat race throw pressure on us, ...and you know in the back of your mind that there's more to life than this, a bigger purpose waiting for you out there, there's something out there that you'd happily jump out of bed for every morning but you just can't put your finger on it eh.....?

For some, it's getting harder to stay sane on this planet because the world's going mad, ...greed, power, corruption, ever increasing living expenses and an ever increasing need for social media, reality tv, valium, alcohol or drugs to get through their day. Most people have given up chasing dreams because they never eventuate anyway, they're too hard or expensive, they lack the knowhow and really just can't be bothered finding a mentor. It's sad how we lose that drive. There's more than enough money, food, industry and trade to go round, our food waste and production is out of control, not to mention general waste. We have continual duplication of trades and industry all competing against each other, capitalism they call it, and most of our local and national politicians are too interested in making sure they'll get voted in on a high pay pack rather than making a difference.

The information in this book has been racking my brain for years, though i know it's not just from me, …..it's another message being channeled from those helping us out, keeping an eye on us, to be filtered among those who are searching for more answers. I kept putting off writing this book for a number of reasons: i felt i wasn't ready, i hadn't succeeded yet, i don't have the credentials or reputation to back up my beliefs, my mates probably think i've gone mad ….lol, and every other reason as to why i shouldn't write it but one night after watching a si-fi series that kept calling out to me i received a kick in the ass to start writing, and wrote the foundation of this book in a couple days, i couldn't keep up with the pen as the information flowed, and it felt exciting, it felt right, it reminded me of my favourite author Neale Donald Walsch.

There have been plenty of books already written over the years covering the same content, and there'll be more to come, ...all have a different flavor or tune, that catch a different eye but send a similar message, and this one will attract a certain audience also, one that stems from my network, then reaches out to those that need it, ...and now that it's found you i hope you find it interesting and it helps you find some of your own answers or inspires you to start thinking about life a bit more. Just keep an open mind, you'll find a message, a seed leading you on to something bigger.

I'm not wanting to be too serious, though some of the content goes deep, ...i talk about love and spiritual ideas, stuff that you wouldn't normally hear about from a bloke like myself, ...so take from it what you want, what feels right for you, just be open minded, ...and remember these are my thoughts and ideas, ...my take on life, with the help from those looking over us, …..so i'm not going to reference my ideas or statements, take it on board or don't, whatever feels right for you.

For the critics and naysayers this is a point of view, my beliefs, what feels good to me as i've already mentioned, dumnified to try and make sense of it all, without holding a degree in quantum physics, economics, theology, medicine, or education but simply my take, through what i've experienced, read, heard, theorize and most importantly feel. The book hasn't been professionally edited, i chose not to, i want it to sound like who i am, not someone else using corrected English. You may find a few profanities, references to drugs & alcohol, bad humour, bad grammar and punctuation, and you may even see a few contradictions, because what i'm writing at times and what i believe i know are two different things, by this i mean the spiritual me knows that all is perfect right now but the physical me gets pissed off and caught up in conspiracies and this 3D illusion we call life.

As a lot of us are becoming aware on this

planet, it's brought the human race through a loop of faith. Our world's indigenous and ancient cultures were extremely in tune with this planet and other forces at play, ...but over time, in my opinion, religion and greed has blurred and deliberately confused these gifts, to a point we don't know what to believe. I grew up going to church every Sunday and praying and all that but to be honest it never felt right, it always felt really fake to me. I remember praying all the time but thinking God isn't even listening, he's not answering any of my prayers, i'm still not rich, my brother's still in pain, mum's still sad, bla bla bla. I looked at others in the church who were crying, speaking in tongues and all that stuff, and as a young bloke it baffled me, is this all just a con, ...but i just went with it. I was even baptised in open water in my early teens and still not fully getting it, even at that point, ...i just went with it because that's what mum wanted. And when people in the church died, became ill, or had accidents, or reverted to drugs, alcohol and other bad stuff, ...as a litter fella i'd ask, "why does God let this stuff happen if he loves us so much...?" Mum would always say either, "he's just teaching him/her a lesson" or "they've allowed the devil to get to them" .....that would annoy the shit out of me cause it didn't make sense. Again, some find peace and comfort in churches and God in churches, but in my case i found him through Neale Donald Walsch's books, so thanks Neale in case you ever read this.....lol.

During my later years of school i got bullied because of a number of reasons which aren't for this book, but one being that i was taught to turn a cheek, great church teachings, ...in my opinion worse thing you could teach a kid, it turned me into a wuss, to not stand up for myself, lacking confidence and self esteem, ...to be honest i don't know how i got through some of those years, i know through the worst i just didn't want to be here, this rock was hell but i stuck it out and even though i prayed every day i felt God never answered me, ...i would just hide in a corner and cry my eyes out at times abusing God. There's a whole lot more to this, and if either of my brothers ever read this book, they'll know what i'm talking about, and they also have their own stories, as we all do but it's not for this book, maybe another time. I'm sure we all could write a book on our upbringings.

I saw others around me suffering the same, and know millions are going through it now as you read this for all sorts of reasons. I now know why and where it comes from, and it's really no one's fault, just the luck of the draw on who your parents are, who your mates are, adults around you and how you're brought up from a physical standpoint, ...but actually it's not the luck of the draw in a spiritual sense, ...there's my first contradiction, ...lol.

My parents loved us dearly and always did what they could to make us happy but they had their own shit going on and were also brought up in a certain way, ...and i'm not going further into all this now but will later, ...not about me but about parents, friends, mentors, etc.

My dad passed away at an awesome age of 95, drank and smoked most of his life, so there goes a couple myths, ...he was never ill until right at the end when he was simply bored and ready to leave. He was a great man who taught me to be humble and stress less, for which i'm still learning, …..thanks pop. Mum's still around as i write this, aged 91, loves a sip too. From mum i have an adventurous spirit, …..thanks mum. I'm grateful for all their love they shared over the years in their own ways.

As a reader i'm open to you having questions and points of view or beliefs, ……we never stop learning and i don't profess to know it all, this is just what works for me from a standpoint of where i'm at right now, so i would love to hear your thoughts and feelings, to connect, which can help me on my journey, …….but i'm not open to abuse or pointless criticism which helps no one, …..turn the abuse into a conversation and i'm happy to chat. My contact details are at the rear of the book, so thanks again and i hope you enjoy the read.

Cheers, Paul.

THE JOURNEY

True Path is a journey leading you in your best feeling direction, the path your soul is trying to guide you along, to become aware and find your path of peace, …….happiness, …….fulfillment, and purpose, ……the reason you came to this beat up but gorgeous planet. At the same time the physical you is trying to lead it's own way because it thinks it knows better, …..you think you can find your own way out of the jungle onto your 'yellow brick road', …..but getting into alignment, finding your purpose, your mission, a part play in the *Bigger Picture* can be harder than you think, and probably isn't along the path you're on right now. Why, because we have been trained over the years to make decisions according to our beliefs and experiences, rather than listen to our intuition, our soul, …..further on this in later chapters.

So what's it all for ….you know, life here….? Deep down you know there's something more to life out there, that takes courage, is exciting, adventurous, that's always calling out to you but you keep discarding it, putting it off, ……not the right time, too busy, don't have the money, bla bla bla, …..everyone has that going on, but only a few follow it. Some have put themselves into a position that makes it hard to follow, (ie) family, job, money, but there's always a path through the jungle to that 'yellow brick road', …..to start helping those on the street, assisting neglected or abused animals, giving aid to victims of war or abuse, standing up for our diminishing rights, starting a business of some sort, becoming self sufficient with finances or food or health, or simply finding some space or time to chill or travel or a change in lifestyle out of the rat race. Whatever it is, generally it'll be of a good nature, good in the physical and ethical sense.

Good feeling thoughts and desires are the exits of our jungle, out of the rat race to start you on your 'yellow brick road', being the life where you can't wait to wake up every morning. It doesn't matter who you are, everyone has a purpose, that's why you came to this planet in the first place. Regardless how trivial or unimportant it may seem, it's important to you and it's important to the growth of humanity somewhere in the puzzle of evolution, the bigger picture of our evolvement as a race, …..and by achieving or attempting that desire you will grow and continue further along your 'yellow brick road', then creating a desire for something new after that, and something new after that, and so the journey continues, ...and that's pretty much the meaning to life here on Earth, finding what makes you happy, grateful, living a purpose, ...and you thought it would be something complicated.....lol. In turn these passions will finance you, feed you, take you wherever you'd love to go, meet the partner you've been desiring, or simply enjoy the journey on your own, whatever your desires, ...in short it's happiness you're following, happiness before planned outcome or practicality or being realistic, ...it's scary and takes courage.

My current purpose is to sow seeds of wisdom through this book and chat to people to find out what part of the jungle they're in, what are they finding tough, what's holding them back, pissing them off, stopping them from living their true life's purpose. Everyone loves a chance to vent and dream, no matter what background or type of person. Not only that, i feel my gift is to see what's behind the closed doors, ...i see their soul, their true identity and let them know. Do i wish to earn a dollar from doing this, absolutely, do i wish to have fun doing this, absolutely, do i wish to travel to all parts of the world doing this, absolutely, …..so i can also focus on my own growth to help lead others along the same path, that's my passion, my purpose, …..what's yours….?

When people open up i feel them on a soul level, …..i feel their hurt, their pain or cry for help and it burns my heart, but i get excited that i have an opportunity to help them find their way out of the jungle. In the past i chose to walk past these conversations, not get involved, …..i didn't want to get involved in a pity party. We all love a good vent and we've all got our own shit going on, our own grievances and i had enough of my own shit going on let alone helping others sort their's out, …..plus my 'man barrier' or ego prevented me from getting a bit warm & fuzzy unless it was for a mate or close family, …..stupid eh. I now know it doesn't take much energy to listen and help people find some hope again, in fact it revitalises me, making me feel good about helping another human out, regardless of culture, beliefs or sex, and who knows where that butterfly effect will take them and others, what that seed may grow into, what ah ha moment it may cause, igniting a decision that's been laying dormant for years, …..it's exciting.

Most people play out life with a front, an act or false identity to protect them from the incoming. My son Callum calls it the 'Man Barrier', ……he even acts it out, putting on a deep voice, arms out, saying "she'll be right mate!"……lol.

I often wondered why people put on fronts, acting like jerks or bullies, being arrogant or quiet and introverted, …..what causes all these different personalities? These fronts prevent us from showing pain, from showing weakness or emotion or tearing up. I lived with them for years, most of us do. For blokes the 'man barrier' camouflages our true face, hides who we really are or what we're feeling deep down so we can be accepted by society, our peers, our mates, ...but have you ever noticed how great it is to find someone on your real level to chat to, where you feel comfortable being yourself rather than playing out someone else, you can have that open conversation about stuff you don't normally talk about, it doesn't happen often but you know those people i'm talking about, you click with them and feel you've known them for years, ...well you have but i won't go there just yet.

So now i let people open up and be vulnerable if they have the courage, and i'm open to listen and they generally let it all hang out. I'm there as an ear only, ...no judgement goin on or criticism or opinion at all, simply a non-judgemental ear. I'm amazed at what people are dealing with and have done so for years. A lot of people are just sick and tired of their current situation, or have been through some shit times and can't explain why it happened, or want to know how they can move on to a brighter future, or find the courage to be more adventurous or confident, to find their next level in the game of life here on Earth, to stop following the herd and find their 'EXIT' sign in their jungle leading them on to their 'yellow brick road' to a life of purpose.

If you feel that you're in a jungle start by turning off tv, quit wasting hours on social media to see who's getting their hair cut, stop reading crap, listening or watching the news, ...it's all crap and you'll hear about it from others anyway. Have a think about what's getting programmed into your head the majority of the day, what are you thinking about, …..start tuning in to good feeling thoughts, listen to audio's like Louise Hay or Esther Hicks, which will immediately change negative thinking into positive thinking, …..if you like tv watch something with meaning or positive, change your social media network to those that you look up to, who seem happy in life, focused on getting ahead, achieving goals, have drive, or mentors that you relate to, that you get excited about listening to. Yes i know it's hard but that's the challenge, creating new habits is always hard, you need to scratch the old record, delete the old life style and create new habits like reading, walking, a hobby, yoga or martial arts or exercise, a club, healthy cooking, whatever tickles ya fancy, …..take out quiet time to write down some goals or things you're grateful for, or simply find some great music to meditate to like Wayne Dyer's 'I AM', and zone out for 20 minutes a day, ……enjoy meditation, it's these quiet times when soul talks to you, it'll be exciting what comes out and it may lead somewhere, like a book......lol. Watch a movie or series that calls out to you, most movies or similar have been channeled to the writer for a reason, they all have a message in there somewhere, ...messages are sent to you everywhere, ...radio, tv, FB, emails, friends, strangers, numbers, ...by all means, just be on the lookout for them and apply them to your life, it gets exciting when you hear or see something that you know is speaking to you. Do i still watch crap on tv occasionally, yes of course, do i still waste time on social media at times, yes of course, they're hard habits to break and i never said i was out of my jungle, i'm certainly still on my journey but it's getting more exciting by the day.

This brings me to my journey, ...it's still becoming, or unbecoming as Holly would say, ...but your journey is forever, there is no destination, it's only ever about the journey, about making it fun and purposeful, leaving you in a place of peace and feeling happy. I found my 'yellow brick road', it was hidden behind a thick jungle of life's crap like most, ...life's crap being some of the people i looked up to for advice, associated with, the fake goals i had that were money driven, old ideas and ideals about me and others, and so on. Recognising all this stuff is called an awakening, becoming aware, as before that time you are purely treading the mill, playing out the game of life without any meaning most of the time. After your awakening the journey here on Earth really starts, and you could be at any stage or age in your life when this happens. It's like awakening from a long sleep, you feel like Neo at the start and then it evolves from there. You may wake up from reading this book, and if so, ...awesome, welcome to the start of your journey! Do i still have stuff going on, absolutely, and always will, when you're low you grow. We are always growing, the more you learn the more you realise how much you don't know. I still lose sight of the path or fall off the side from time to time but that's ok, now i recognize when i do and jump back on as quick as i can, knowing that each trip-up is another lesson that i will never return to, ...being non-aware, it's simply impossible to do that, ...once aware you can't go back, like Neo in the Matrix, you can't reverse the process. I know what to look out for now, the signs, the messages, what to listen out for, and i know i have soul guiding me in the right direction. Now it's just about learning to let go, listen and watch for the signs, and trust that process. I let go knowing that soul's got it sorted, soul's got my back so whatever happens is just meant to be, and simply believe it to be so. This may sound corny or difficult in times of turmoil but after you've done it a couple times you'll look back and see that it does turn out ok, so keep doing it every time you start worrying, ...whether it's bills, health, friendships, work, whatever, ...simply take a deep breath, relax and tell soul to sort it out, and know it'll work out just fine, just be in the moment and try not to be anything else, ...99% of worries never happen, the 1% will teach you something, and you'll still be alive in the morning, the sun will still rise, people will still be doing their thing, most unaware of your issues. See yourself out in the solar system, looking back at Earth, how miniscule you are in comparison with everything going on around the planet, ...it puts into perspective our issues most of the time.

Obviously you will still go through difficult times, so be present in those moments, feel the pain, the stress, the sadness, whatever it is feel it, but also know that soul will show you a way out when you're ready to move past that event, when you've learnt what you needed to learn from it, and the journey continues on.

I'm not here to profess that i know it all, that i know life's answers, jsut create a simple 101 easy read to get you started on finding your true path, to recognise or make sense of your crap and the world of personal development as they call it.

So, who am i, ...born at a young age, didn't enjoy school, employed in police, army, and building & construction, ...ran a couple businesses, ...lost our house and net wealth among other things, ...dusted off and moved to the country, ...drove trucks and jumped back on the tools building for a bit, ...climbed the corporate ladder to a couple manager roles. As i write this book, i run a building maintenance business with my son Callum, with a view of getting back into property investing & reno's whilst running some type of a mentor program, helping those that want to be helped. I've just finished up as a trainer & assessor for people wanting to drive trucks, ...i'm 51, sort of quit full time smoking after 25yrs, still enjoy a rollie on occasions, stay fairly fit & healthy, swear a lot and enjoy a beer, …..got a pretty open mind and feel i'm going through a fair change in life right now, …..i tell my wife it's metamorphosis….lol….she's not sure about the butterfly thing though, more like a moth. I've travelled quite a bit, worldwide and Australia, …..enjoy outdoor activities and sports but want time to do more, ……i've bungied, jumped out of planes, played with all sorts of weapons and can swing a hammer among other tools and trades.

I'm proud of my achievements, …..i've tried a lot of stuff, some of it to seek fulfillment and purpose and some just for fun, but it never ends, …..i haven't found that happy place yet, where i wake up in the morning excited about the day ahead, where i'm naturally at peace and happy, without being on holiday in paradise or drinking…..lol, some of you may relate, …..but i feel closer as the days role on. I do enjoy being on the tools and seeing the finished products but it's not on my own properties, it's still trading time for money. In the meantime i just keep listening and learning and following the messages to become more aware. I've had an adventurous life with a lot more to come, done and experienced some crazy shit, like a lot of us have, ...the lessons learned along the way will help me find the path to stay and tackle the jungle in case i stray.

I've been with my gorgeous wife for over 30 yrs, have 2 kids, boy and girl who have turned out to be incredible souls, i look up to them so much, hearts of gold, placed into our lives for a reason, to straighten me out, ...and it's working.

Writing this book feels right but it's a bit out of my comfort zone, ...you know, making it public who i'm being now. My jungle is believing and having confidence with who i am and where i'm going, …..choosing to live in alignment, with integrity and being real. I wish to use my life experiences to follow a path that has always been there for me, ……listening, coaching, writing, potentially working overseas building shelters for those in need, and helping people get out of their struggle zones, who knows where that'll take me, let's wait 'n' see what the universe has in store, …..it may be nothing like what i envisage but i'm excited and hope it involves a challenge, beaches and warm weather…..lol.

After we lost our house and all and i stopped feeling sorry for myself and sobered up, i got stuck into books and PD, trying to figure it all out, ….you know, the meaning of life. I came across a book trilogy called Conversations With God by Neale Donald Walsch, or rather it found me. I read it and i woke up, became aware of who i am, ….i can remember sitting in bed becoming more aware with the more i read, and i haven't looked back since, it was an awesome feeling that i felt i knew the meaning of life here on Earth. Whether true or not, that didn't matter, it felt right for me, it all made sense, …..church, God, law of attraction, the bible, war, the 'Man Barrier', grog, smokes, the human body, losing my house, …..everything made sense, it was a pretty cool feeling, …..but then i realised there was so much i didn't know about the universe and wanted to know, where do i find the answers to all my questions now.

At the time we were broke, financially and mentally broken, …….we'd lost everything, including my dignity and pride and found out what being depressed, alone and failing felt like, …..at times questioning why the hell i was here, as it didn't make any sense prior to reading the book, ……."if this is life i don't want to play no more". I'd worked my ass off, always had money and thought everything was ticking along just fine but the shit hit the fan real quick, material possessions gone along with my confidence, and it took us so long to get to where we were. I'd caused us to be homeless, my wife and two young kids, who relied on me as their bread winner and i'd failed them. I can lay blame to others but in short it was my doing, it was always going to happen anyway, backing me into a corner so i would experience failure and search to find that book, to wake up, hear my soul, and i'm glad it did, …..i still read and listen to that trilogy today among others.

And there began, the rabbit warren, Pandora's box of the universe opened for me, my awakening, becoming aware and realising what little i really knew, and when you think you know, you realise you don't really know at all because there's always another level. I look back at my way of thinking prior to my awakening and it was like i was living the life of a zombie with lack of understanding and awareness and direction, my only purpose was to pay bills and drink beer, ...which at times was fun but becomes frustrating not knowing what it's all for.

When you think your goal is to get that job, or buy that house, or reach that financial status, or find that partner, you'll always have that next goal, ...physically, mentally and spiritually, no matter where you are in life, that's it, no destination, **it's simply a journey to find happiness**. We're like plants, if we're not thriving or being nurtured we're wilting or dying, crying out for some lovin, a purpose to live, and a lot of the time looking for some guidance or direction, ...mentors. That's not to say you can't have material riches or cars or whatever it is that you want but it's how much you enjoy the process of getting them that's important, how happy you are along the way, and then how happy you'll be when you get them before you move onto your next goal. T. Harv Eker is a great mentor for money along with spirituality, which most don't believe go together but they do, it's all in your thought processes and subconscious, …..your belief system. But, if these items aren't making you happy then it's not the possessions you're after, rather, an underlying need for fulfillment and purpose being temporarily satisfied by the material items, the same as what i've experienced by trying so many different things. You don't need to bust your ass by working 5-7 days, or get the highest paid job, ……simply learn to get in tune with soul and find your 'yellow brick road', it will make the game more fun and exciting when on your true path, your happy place, and the things that you enjoy will come in abundance with little or no effort, depending how in tune you are. This goes for those struggling to even live, for those in jail, on drugs, alcohol and so on, ……they're all temporary remedies to plug a hole, …..lack of love or purpose or understanding of how to find happiness again. We were all born happy little kiddies but shit happens along the way and for some it becomes quite painful, to a point where it's unbearable, …..drugs, alcohol and crime are used to simply bear life, ……sad but true. And to make it even worse a lot of society label users & abusers as losers but know this, there is a way out, and i'm here to help those that are keen to try. I'm here to help those wanting to be involved in the bigger picture find that path.

So what is the **bigger picture**…….?

THE BIGGER PICTURE

I say *bigger picture* because i don't really know what the *big picture* is, it's beyond my current human brain capacity while in physical form but the *bigger picture* to me is where everyone is in alignment with their true soul purpose here on Earth, living a physical 3D existence that's truly fun, has purpose, and leads to growth and awareness of all that exists here on Earth, which leads to living a 5D existence. I believe the big picture involves the bigger picture and it extends to all existence, which i can only leave to your limited imaginations, and i don't say limited in a derogatory way, it's just that you have to agree, we as humans don't really know a hell of a lot outside our own lives and life on this planet. We have become accustomed to a life and culture within a system that has been created over thousands of years as we've evolved, and this culture is how we currently live, think and speak. Some say it's been influenced over the years by the rich and wealthy, the religious elite, and other powerful entities, …..i'll leave that to your imagination and beliefs. Think about where most of our laws and customs have come from, who they serve the most, how our ideas and systems have changed over the years to suite those that benefit the most. Even though we have some great minds and qualified people to help us understand what's out there, how to live, what to eat, etc, …..most of it is guess work, other is influenced, made redundant, illegal or immoral through greed, …..again my opinion. It's hard to know what to listen to or who to follow or believe these days. I operate on what feels good, …..if i hear a conspiracy or theory and it feels good to me, I'll accept that there is a good chance of it being possible, no matter who it comes from or their qualification or credentials, …..but we, as numerous societies around the world don't operate like this, we generally make decisions on personal gain or greed, …..we have a long way to go before we truly live with integrity.

I feel we have come a little way over the time we've occupied this planet, even though it's just a blink of an eye to mother Earth. In that short time though we've behaved like a bunch of shit heads, spoiled kids, bullies, …..smashing our toys, taking as many of the cookies out of the jar as we can, pushing the weaker ones out of the sand pit or play pen, …..yes i know i'm generalising, that's not everyone but i'm gonna say a majority. When humans get an opportunity to make money, claim land, follow fortune, rule over others, take control, murder, influence, destroy, pillage, disempower, allow *Ego* to flow, …..be sure they'll do it. Look at the influence govts, religions, beliefs and cults have on society, …..they've influenced wars, human atrocities and disgraceful acts, even towards our planet's indigenous who were so in tune with this planet prior to white fella's greed, rules, religions and govt powers coming along. We've got groups stripping our magnificent rainforests for $$$, 2 football fields every 3 mins in the Amazon alone, ……inhumane slaughter of animals, …..land & sea, having no regard or remorse for cruelty, and yes i'm a meat eater. Our govt's and regulators taxing and enforcing rules that have humanity tied up into their palms, creating stress and illness, which in turn creates violence and dismay, …..people are ready to explode. Once upon a time govt's would govern the peoples choices but now they're a power unto their own, …..and then there's the untouchables, corruption and secrets throughout those powers, including the military and elite groups, ….massive corporations leading the world with money and greed, with no transparency and little care for humanity. I'm not gonna go into the use of marijuana as a healing herb or useful material, or the over use of fossil fuels, the ever growing pharmaceutical industry, the hoarding of gold, power behind the elite, fluorides and chlorine in our water, vaccines, water theft, fake wars, and so on, …..we've certainly tied ourselves up into knots, like a 'birds nest' on a fishing reel, it'll take some time to undo but I feel we have to start somewhere. Simple awareness is a start, we should stop ignoring the facts and begin to call out the elite powers and support those making a stand towards transparency.

That's my rant, my belief in where i think we

are as a race right now, ...are there decent human beings, groups and govt leaders doing the right thing, ...absolutely. Have we made some incredible feats of technology, medicine, industry and so on, ...absolutely. Understandably, our industries need to house billions, feed billions, clothe billions, and that's constant, so to come up with better systems that deliver unpolluted water and fresh food to the billions 24/7 without chems will take some work and not simply a switch over to hydroponics or total organic, I get that. We in the free world must be grateful for having everything at our fingertips, hot & cold water, massive variety of food, clothing, housing, transport, world travel, and freedom to roam pretty much anywhere. Pretty crazy to think how good we really have it, ...like, what goes in to simply having a can of tuna on the shelf of the supermarket, ...steel produced and transported to manufacture the can, labeling, further transport to the tuna factory, the tuna farmed and processed to go inside the can, and then transported once again to the supermarkets, …..all for about $2, …..crazy! So i'm not pointing the finger as i haven't done jack shit towards preventing half of this stuff, it's purely an observation and wake up call for all of us. If we all start shaking the tree the snake will fall out eventually.

Being grateful is important. It'll certainly help bring you abundance of the good stuff, …..wealth, health, and happiness, …..i know sometimes it's hard to be grateful if the bills are mounting up or you're not working, or ill or separating from a partner, or in jail, or whatever, …..but to be consciously grateful will turn things around for you bit by bit, …..what have you got to lose….? Start listening to positive stuff when you can, write down 5 things daily that you're grateful for, …..and you'll start seeing some changes for the better, and the hardest one for some is to show love for everyone and everything, …..sounds corny but it works.

I have to constantly remind myself that we are in a great space, it just needs refining. I feel people are becoming more aware today and some are taking incredible action to help move us forward in the right direction which does make a difference and does eventually influence or rub off on our world leaders, to gradually improve our understanding of us as the human race, the inhabitants of this planet which is our only one at the moment for a few miles out there, …..to rid society of the bullies bit by bit, …..damn…..i'm just to blame with some of my history with army, police, and having old style thinking in the past. Again i'm not pointing the finger, i'm just pointing out as a race we could probably do a bit better nurturing our backyards. And yes, we've heard all this before, ……..I believe my role on this rock is to help bring awareness to the tougher sorts, the ones that say it's all a load of crap, she'll be right mate, but deep down they know there's something more out there, more they could do. So if you're reading this book, regardless of who you are or what you think, it's not a coincidence, …..it's been placed in your hands, so begin to think about why and the role you could play in this, your short visit here on Earth is for a purpose, look for it, ….it's not just about you, as much as you are the most important human on the planet, so is everyone else.

Now let's go pretty deep for a bit. Earlier i mentioned we live in a 3D world, but some of us are teaching ourselves to reach a 5D reality. So what's the difference, and what does it mean to live this way. Before i go into this i want to say that if you think of all life as energy, atoms if you like, some vibrating quickly, some slowly, …..you can even see this under a powerful microscope, so i'm not making this up.

A rock or tree vibrates slower than a human body, hence you can't really see them moving except they are. A human body slower than fire, fire slower than thought. Thought could be said to be 4D. As the dimensions increase so does the frequency or vibration, like radio waves. As a human, most are coded or tuned to vibrate at around 10Hz, which falls within the 3D frequency, …..i'll explain where you receive your codes from shortly. Just so you know, Earth vibrates at about 432Hz, so if you wish to brighten up your day listen to some 432Hz music.

You can alter your coding, using modern day Shamans or other qualified specialists, …..they get rid of unwanted codes that pick up on or attract low vibrating frequencies, poverty and sadness for example, then re program you with higher vibrating codes for attracting wealth, happiness and success, etc. It's a lot more complicated than that as there's so many factors that effect your frequency and coding. These new codes are like tuning in a radio to the right frequency, being through our minds, which i'll explained later. This then allows you to learn to vibrate at the appropriate frequency and with practice you can install codes to attract fulfillment, love, purpose, etc. The higher you go the better the experience, generally during meditation. Some Buddhist monks spend their whole life practicing to meditate to high levels of vibration, reaching higher levels of reality/dimensions, some even leaving our 3D, 4D & 5D world, slipping away into ascension, 6D and upwards, …..again if interested do some research.

I hope some of this made sense, maybe read

it a few times, but if you see us like a radio that could be coded, which they can be, ...and the radio vibrates as it's frequency goes up, eventually shattering glass and beyond. That's the easiest example i can think of. So lets have a go at understanding the various dimension.

1D Reality (1st dimension) - is a dot, no up, down, dimension or depth.

2D Reality (2nd dimension) - is like a picture on a wall, no depth, simply flat. If you lived in a 2D world and hit a fence which would simply be a line as you wouldn't see height, you wouldn't be able to go over it, only around.

3D Reality (3rd dimension) - is the dimension that most of humanity lives in here on Earth, including animal life. They are aware of length, width and depth, which includes height and breadth, through our 5 senses which are used to create our awareness of these dimensions – sight, hearing, smell, taste & touch. Some say that this is purely an illusion, a perception and no more, but you can do your own research on this topic. I personally believe this myself, but also believe that we can alter that perception to experience this 3D reality in whatever way we want, as it's simply a game if you like, you can go up the levels.

4D Reality (4th dimension) - is 3D with the extra dimension of time or imagination. We experience 4D every day when we sleep. Some of us have also developed the ability to have lucid dreams and out of body experiences (OBEs), and these for the most part take place in 4D. Others routinely access 4D through meditation. Sometimes when you dream you can hear, feel and see things. Your imagination/mind doesn't know whether this is real or not, until you wake up back into 3D reality. Now 5D is the next level again, and the final one for this book.

5D Reality (5th dimension) - *Article by Crystal Compton / Metaphysical* (edited).

This is where things start to get a little weird, so hang on. 5D is the realm of Light and Love. It is the plane of Christ Consciousness and the Ascended Masters (Buddha, Abraham, Jesus, if you believe in any of them). When we talk about heaven, we are talking for the most part about 5D which is a land of complete timelessness, supreme illumination, and bliss, ...which is everywhere, even here on Earth. I have personally experienced 5D and to explain the sensation or experience would be like trying to explain the feeling of extreme love or an orgasm.

However, only parts of heaven are experienced in 5D. Heaven actually extends beyond just one dimension (and even density), but for our purposes it does start in the 5th. And, within the 5th, there are many portals that quickly and seamlessly grant access to higher levels of existence, (ie) 6D is said to be where Jesus went upon ascension.

If we are to Ascend directly from 3 to 5, as some spiritual teachers say, we will have to first go through the lowest-rungs of 5D, which is the proverbial basement. By the way there is no bad connotation when calling it a basement. In fact the 5D basement will feel like unimaginable ecstasy to us!

It is in these lower levels of 5D that we will be processed after death, experiencing things like the holographic life review and Restoration. Once processing is over we will move on to higher 5D levels. Very few teachers can speak correctly on the highest levels of 5D and beyond because truly, not many have experienced it and also there are no human words that adequately describe it.

Here is a secret about 5D: It is the level of jumping. Jumping is when we, through a vibratory process and sometimes completely randomly, skip the need for incremental ascension through the dimensions, and instead access dimensions out of order, and can even leave the density itself.

The density is the house in which all the dimensions exist. And, there are many houses.

'In my Father's house are many mansions, and I go to prepare a place for you. —John 14:2'

Soooo, that got deep, but it's a great one to read more about if you're so inclined. I find it fascinating, especially after visiting 5D that one time, and to some it all sounds like a complete load of shit. Take it as it makes you feel, and do you really care what anyone thinks.

I believe we are here to follow a plan that is bigger than all of us but involves all of us, …..it's just that not everyone is aware or ready to take on the challenge. It isn't one of hardship or influence or persuasion, though it will take courage at times, ….it's one of happiness, peace, purpose, transparency and fun. When you're in a place like that you feel pretty awesome right, ……imagine being in that place every day, …..that's being in alignment with who you are, having true integrity, your true purpose, …….that's your goal in this Earth game, ……not worrying, not being ill with disease, not fighting, not being afraid or lonely or lost. There's a lot of guides out there offering their assistance, physically and spiritually, …..the closest of them is soul. It will guide you to your feel good path, your journey, your part to play in the bigger picture, …..the bigger picture is a journey of a larger consciousness, a collective consciousness, to bring all of humanity into alignment but there's no deadline or urgency or expiry date, it's just you having fun while having the courage to take on your purpose here on Earth. If you chose to do this we just need to teach you how to listen to soul who is your guide, who is part of a collective of souls or guides if you like.

You've been chosen to take on this mission, that's why you as a sperm beat millions of other sperms at that pretty critical moment, ……you got to the front door first, you got the only seat in the house when the music stopped, you were born a winner!

Even though everyone is connected to soul, and everyone has a mission, it doesn't mean that every person becomes aware while here this time. Some go on living in their non-remembering trance of basic life on Earth, ……..working, playing, stressing, watching tv, listening to media and watching others live their journey, like watching the footy, …..then growing old and dying, …….and at the same time some people without becoming aware live fantastic lives, fulfilling, purpose driven and add to humanity in some way without even knowing they've done that. The difference is you've now become aware, and will consciously choose your path, one of courage that leads to happiness and purpose, or one that seems easier but ends up being more stressful and harder as you won't be in alignment with your soul purpose, and that's maybe where you're at right now, but it's temporary.

Everyone has a kind heart, it's just some hide it well, in fear of being hurt or seen as weak, so a lot of people wear a front they can't get rid of and die wearing it……sad yeah, this prevents them from becoming aware, they refuse or ignore the signs but that's ok too, just love em and don't spend too much time with them,......regardless of who they are, who knows, you may even be sleeping with one....lol.

The ones that aren't aware or ready to un-become, or to re-member probably won't understand what you're up to, ...trust me, you'll experience this with friends and family once you're on your path, it's quite funny really, ...some of the faces and comments you get if you talk about this stuff and they're not ready to hear it, ...but then another time you'll start up a conversation with a total stranger and feel you've known them forever, as they're so on the same wave length, seeking their own path, and the conversation feels so awesome and inspiring and exciting, you want it to last forever, it's like you have God sitting with you while you talk to each other, ...they're the conversations i love, ...i've got goose bumps just thinking about it. It's never a coincidence that you meet up with these people, as both of you have a message to pass on to each other, a further hint for the riddle, …..it's cool stuff.

So, the trance we were born into was deliberate, it is designed for you to experience becoming aware, re-membering, ……my coach and author Holly Nunan calls it 'Unbecoming', ……it is learning about who you really are, reading books, finding the signs, learning new exciting facts, trying some weird stuff like listening to your soul and learning to decipher your *ego* voice from your own voice (*spirit*) from *soul* voice. Learning and practicing this stuff is fun, figuring out that most humans really don't know much about themselves. In a way you feel like NEO, Indiana Jones, Angelina Jole, looking for the treasure of fun, freedom, peace and purpose, whatever that is for you, meanwhile starting to play out your part in the bigger picture, but you need a guide and map through the jungle to get there. The jungle is full of traps, …..alcohol, drugs, crime, violence, self doubt, and all the other crap going on in your life that you don't want.

While all this is going on, the ego voice in your head is doubting your path, your beliefs, what you read, ……hell even this book, but ask yourself ….."does it feel right, does it feel good, is it exciting, is it for the good of humanity in some way?" The option is to throw this book down and go watch tv, cos that'll get you further…lol.

So those voices in your head, how many are there, where do they come from, am i just going mad or losing it? Again, these are my beliefs, not fact, not gospel but what feels right for me, ….go with what feels right for you.

There are 3 main voices: **spirit**, **soul** and **ego**, ...i'm keeping it simple because it's not that simple.   All 3 are discussed in more detail later.

Spirit - that loud voice, the one talking to yourself all the time, whether out loud or thinking, that's you as your non-physical self but as a human, like animals, we have the capabilities to create what we know as sound by blowing air through our vocal cords, vibrating to churn out sounds that we've learned to tune into a language(s) that we understand to communicate. But the initial thought comes from spirit, in our non-physical source energy self, …….. it is you, always will be you, and always has been you. Another form of communication is ESP but i'll let you do your own research on that one too. So if what i am saying feels right to you then you could only begin to imagine the possibilities of spirit and thought, …..mind blowing, and beyond my knowledge at this point. When meditating, the peak place to reach is enlightenment, ……it's where you create a straight or physical connection to your non-physical energy source self…..spirit in the 5D.

As i mentioned earlier, one day while driving along a highway i experienced 5D, …..it seemed to last for some time, i visualized my path to take in the short term as clear as watching a movie but the most memorable part was the utmost incredible warm comforting feeling of love and assurance that everything is ok and i'm not alone. When i snapped out of it i immediately started crying due to the overwhelming feeling of love if you like, ……..quite hard to explain but it was an incredible experience that assured me that there is more out there, that there is a God or something looking over us, and when snapping out i just wanted to go back because it felt so good, and i haven't experienced anything like that since. I know the late Stephen Hawkins who had some incredible theories and was an amazing guy, but his theory about there being no God just doesn't feel good or right to me, …..i know with 100% conviction that there's something out there full of love, and i felt it, regardless of who believes what, that is what i believe, that spirit is energy, vibrating, and outright love, and when in tune with it's vibration you feel incredible, ……that's spirit, God……further explained later.

Soul - that all knowing quiet voice that's always there, it's your gut feeling, your intuition, your instinct, your good feeling thoughts, your guide(s). It's that voice that tells you to start playing a musical instrument, to join that club for dancing or martial arts or gym or footy, to take up that hobby, to write that book, …..boom…..lol. To take on that adventure, to try that different restaurant, to ask that guy/gal out, to grab that screw driver as you walk past your tool box, or to say something to someone, or to buy food & drink for the street person as you walk past, or to throw a coin or note into the buskers hat, or to stand up for yourself.....fight rather than flight, and so on, ...but you don't do any of these most of the time do you, because no one up till now has told you that these are soul thoughts, your guide, guiding you, helping you and others in your path. Soul knows all, it knows your path, the YBR, and how to stay on it. Do we always listen to it, no, ...but why not? Because it's a progressive learning habit, the more you do the more you get, the clearer it gets.

Ego - that pain in the ass voice tainted by opinions, beliefs, doubts, false learning's, crappy rules and every other negative thought process that's been planted in there over the years, especially for those that have been through trauma of any kind, they will anchor some serious negative thought patterns. How often do you think of a great idea and then you smash it down with crap thoughts, "it'll never work", "as if he or she will be attracted to you", "why try, you'll probably fail anyway", "imagine what they'll think", bla bla bla….! That's ego. The negative ideas about our life, the way we think of ourself and others, planted in our head, in our memory bank over the years, create our ego, and filter every thought into a perception, an opinion of yourself. We think through these filters every day, every minute, every thought, every conversation, every decision through your whole life. The average human has about 60-80,000 thoughts per day, so image what effect on your life some of this stuff can have over time.

These filters have been created from your parents, teachers, tv, radio, multi media, friends and so on, …..at certain points in our life some of these actually design within us who we are, how we act, our personality, so it's really important as parents or peers to only speak to our young in a positive, uplifting and inspirational way while growing up, as they soak in every piece of information they can, until such a time that person is old enough to start thinking for themselves and making their own decisions, from which they'll make through their filters that you helped create, …….scary yeah, we are so programmed it's not funny, but we can change it, it's not too late, we can change our thought process which will change our path which will change our outlook on life.   These are the codes i mentioned earlier.   Depending on your upbringing, influencers and teachings is what decides your coding and influences your filters. So many people today are coded with slave codes, people pleasing codes, and they don't realize why they are the way they are. What frequencies are you transmitting and what frequencies are you letting through your filters….?

If you're young then you may have less crap programming to delete, unless you've been through trauma, then this takes some work but you can do it. Life here is like playing a video game, as you learn to defeat each section or chapter of the game you move on to the next level, and along the way you get bonuses and extra powers to make it easier to defeat the enemy, 'Ego', that's your enemy. The only difference with the game of life on Earth, there is no destination, no ending, you just keep growing, winning, and occasionally getting pumbled but when you win your bonuses are having fun, being happy, healthy, learning more and experiencing what this planet has to offer, meanwhile re-membering or unbecoming. This continues until your body has had enough, which is a whole other story,

.....more on that later. We can grow from every lesson in life, and these lessons are generally when we're doing it hard, in all forms but look for the next sign, in a book, a movie, chatting to someone or whatever, there'll always be a sign, a hint on how to move to the next level, learning to see them can be the hard part, and when you see them trust in them, have faith that it's for you, follow your soul, your intuition, it never fails to amaze.

BODY

Body – the bag of bones, made up of energy in the form of intelligent cells, all vibrating at a speed that seems to keep us together, not bouncing around like fire or light, though made up of the same stuff, …….everything is made up of the same universal ingredients, just of different variants and vibrating at different speeds, …….our tree's, rocks, water, animals, stars, all just vibrating at different speeds and containing different variants of elements. The human body / vessel has been made up of elements allowing us to breath the air on Earth, walk upright in this era, and consume the food on this planet. We may be different in other places if you believe this could be, …..more on that later.

The main difference between us and animals, as mentioned previously, is that we have free will, other animals have limited will, (ie) eat, root, shit, and moo....yeah i know humans do that too but our free will is pretty much unlimited, we can choose whatever we want to achieve by simply vibrating (transmitting) thought, ...whether growing a piece of fruit or flying to other solar systems, whether creating scientific inventions or using ESP. When we put our mind to anything we create it in thought, in vibration and eventually it will be achieved, ...through thought and faith anything is possible.

Back to body, ...we are made up of tubes, everything in our body is a tube, think about it, bones, veins, lungs, intestines and organs, neurons, hair follicles, even our nerves and electrical conductors, ...all tubes, ...quite fascinating really. I'm not a doctor but it doesn't take a medical degree to realise if any of these tubes become blocked or unhealthy with dis-ease like clots in veins or macular and cataracts dis- ease in eyes, parkinson's or dementia from blocked brain pathways, or even bad bacteria in your intestine tubes or stomach or nasal tubes or throat tubes or lung tubes or ear tubes, and so on, you get the picture. Now, what is more fascinating is the old saying, "you are what you eat", ……there is a fruit or vegetable naturally grown or available on this planet from natural sunlight and water that mimics every organ or tube or set of tubes in our body, (ie) walnut – brain, broccoli – lungs, celery – bones, avocado – womb and uterus, oranges and grapefruit – women's breasts, banana's – you guessed it… willy, carrots – eyes, tomato – heart, clams – testies, ginger – stomach, sweet potatoes – pancreas, even red wine – blood, and many more. Reference for this: Don & Tyler Tolman, amazing father and son, worth going to see live if you get the chance.

So as we already know, fruits and vegies are good for us but they can also be used as a remedy for the relief of relevant dis-ease, it's mother nature's fix on Earth, certainly a better option than toxic man made medicines given out by a medical practitioner, yes that's right, they are practicing on you, as no one truly knows the long term side effects of any pharmaceutical medication, only what's known is that they leave behind a trail of toxins that your body wants to get rid of, and if you keep taking medication to try and cure every dis-ease that your body is naturally trying to cure by vomiting, or diarrhea, or eczema, or psoriasis, or sweating and so on, as this is your body's way of excreting or removing the dis-ease, then your body has no other option than to create a garbage bin to place all these toxins into, (ie) a tumor, and it will generally be placed close to the main area of dis-ease. I realise it's not as easy as i make out to cure dis-ease or illness but i believe there is another major factor causing most dis-ease, from the general cold to major sickness, and that is Law of Attraction, you are what you think, as well as eat but you will create a blockage in whatever area of your body that you're not happy with through thought, ...face, breasts, back, and so on, all relating to something going on in your subconscious, more on this later.

We have natural remedies for most dis-ease and natural nutrients to sustain a healthy body supplied by mother nature herself, just ask the planet's indigenous, who lived on them until white man knew better. Again our thinking has a lot to do with it, using Law of Attraction will greatly assist us in fixing any dis-ease we have, minor to life threatening, you just need to know what's causing it, what hidden factor is creating the blockage, it will be an old dusty trophy stored down in the pool room.....lol. But, what i will put out there is if our cells are intelligent, then yes, we can communicate with them, visualize them being clear tubes, that pure feeling of blood flowing freely, vitamins flowing freely, every flowing like a new plumbing system in a house, clean and unobstructed. I talk to my cells all the time, they're like my workers, keeping this fine tuned machine running, obliterating crap, flushing the system, all that shouldn't be in there is flushed out, also telling me what boosts or backup are needed. Ever had a craving for a water, an apple, a banana, or some obscure fruit or veg, that's your body letting you know it needs a boost for a reason, eat it straight away, then feel them buggers going to work, keeping the machine in tune. Do the same with illness, focus on that area being smashed, spring cleaned by your cells, clearing whatever blockage needs to be cleared, it works every time and i can honestly say that it's rare that i'm ill, even with a cold, there's no need to be! Your car engine doesn't break down unless it's not being service or maintained, it will run for a million miles if you look after it, yes the parts will wear but we're a bit different in that respect, we actually replace our parts within every 3 years, yes that's right, ……our cells replace themselves continually, some quicker than others but the longest is 3 years, and they're in our eyes. An obvious example of this is hair, fingernails and skin, you can see this happen but all the others aren't that obvious. So if we update every 3 years or so why do we carry on illness or a scar or a lost limb for that fact, it's what we believe to be true, we aren't yet in a place on this planet to change that but in extreme cases people, through focus and belief, regain feeling in their legs or arms again, even after a severed spinal cord, people regain sight, hearing and cure severe illness…….it's all around the same principle, thought and belief. Here's another example of what we can do from our thought, which is energy, vibration, ……..look into how water molecules change as we think about them while drinking, you'll be amazed and that's simple science so why wouldn't all the rest be possible, it all relates to energy, vibration, and belief. That there alone should be opening Pandora's Box ….lol, …..our bodies and minds are capable of amazing feats.

It has been said in a number of books that i've read, incl CWG, that the human body is designed to live forever but of course that would entail a whole lot of different thinking and diet and total change in our environment for the human body to live and think clean and to actually believe that it could live that long. We've been taught by recent history, current beliefs and actually seeing that most people leave here after playing out 80-90 years, regardless of what we eat ………what if we ate the right foods and believed with 100% conviction that we'll live to 2-300 years old, would our mind, through vibrating energy, automatically program our body (cells) to make that happen, …..mmm …..food for thought, boom boom …..lol.

On the flip side what do you think drugs, smokes, alcohol, junk food and the like do to us, besides leaving toxins in our system that our cells have to fight off and remove, if that's what your telling them to do, ….yes you can talk to them, they're you, tell them to go to work and strip all that crap from you body and send it to the sewage farm. All this stuff numbs our senses, blocks our intuitive paths, masks or blurs soul's messages, as well as thought and vibration. Yes that's right, in the numbing and blocking and masking process these chemicals and toxins make it harder for us to find our YBR, find our way out of the jungle. They trick us into thinking it's all ok, just one more beer or smoke, it can't hurt but you know as i do, it keeps us from feeling our true beings, being our true selves, it allows Ego in .....big time. It temporarily masks pain and worry, giving us temporary pleasure, a temporary escape from our crap but it's like taking a panadol, it wears off and doesn't cure the dis-ease, reality sets back in and the cycle continues. The only way to remove that dis-ease, that worry or pain is to cleanse our bodies, so they're in tune with what soul is showing us. That's why so many are taking on body and mind cleansing programs, to clear out our tubes of toxins, to allow our body to mend, like running an anti-virus through our program, so we can be in tune to our senses, our soul, and follow those guiding hints of inspiration and signs to find our way out of the jungle onto our YBR. Do i drink, smoke and eat crap, ...yep, and that's my journey through my jungle right now. I've been brought up in that culture and i blame no one, i've made my own choices on my own journey as we all do.

Disclaimer: re above, i don't have any medical qualifications so please seek advice from whomever you feel can assist, a doctor or naturopath or alternative healer, when seeking cures or treatments for illness or dis-ease or the basic ailment. Follow your soul, your intuition on who can benefit you the most. Me personally, i wouldn't go to a standard GP to be practiced on. GP's and specialists are fantastic at finding the issue, most of the time, that's what they've studied and i praise them for that, and i'm sure there's passionate GP's out there that just want to help people re-pair but too many today simply prescribe whatever to get you out of their room for the next patient to rock on in, and i assure you, the waiting rooms are becoming busier by the day. So many people are becoming hypochondriacs, relying on medication to get them through the day, it's really sad but relevant to this book, we've all seen the stats on the placebo effect, it doesn't lie…..these people are lost or bored or just tired, or so that's what they're thinking, so their system is only running at 50%, they're not looking after themselves due to lack of self respect and hope. It actually chokes me up just writing this stuff out, that such a large number of our humans on this planet are like this. The pressures brought on by life getting too fucking hard and stressful, …..financially, through bureaucracy and constant new laws and regulations tying us up into knots, big brother going too far, taxes, ridiculous utility bills, rates, discrimination, racism, religious feuds, housing prices, monopoly industry taking over the little man, greed, …..and people are feeling like pawns, having no say or power to change any of this, our kids simply throw their hands in the air and say, "Well you made this mess…!", sad. Anyway, my point is that stress along with diet is killing a lot of us today. It's funny, animals aren't suffering like this, unless getting shipped overseas, …..thought i'd just throw that one in.

With regards to medication, i personally don't use antibiotics or the like, and haven't done so for years. I may use natural herbal remedy tablets available in your local supermarket or health food stores for a cold or headache, in conjunction with some fruit and plenty of water.

That's pretty much what i needed to say about our body, yes there's much more as it's an amazing feat of the universe in its design, that's evolved over millions of years to become who we are now, assimilated with spirit (breath) and soul (intelligence / mind).

A quick one from Abraham:

"Your sophisticated physical body exists because of the intelligence of your cells. And the intelligence of your cells exists because of their Connection to Source Energy.

When doctors and scientists try to find cures for diseases without taking into consideration the Vibrational relationship between the physical Being and Source Energy, they are looking for cures in all the wrong places. If the resistance that disallowed the Well-Being to begin with is not released, it will show up in the form of another and another disease.

Your cells, because of their connection to the intelligence of Source Energy, know exactly what to do in order to become the incredible variety of functioning cells in your magnificent physical body. And in the absence of the hindrance that is caused by your resistant negative thought, that communication stays open to clear, up-to-the-moment interaction, keeping your physical body at peak and perfect performance.

In the absence of negative emotion—and therefore the allowance of complete alignment and communication with Source Energy—your physical body can reclaim its balance and recover from any imbalance. And once balance has resumed, it is easy to maintain with consistently good-feeling thoughts."

Excerpted from Getting into the Vortex Guided Meditation CD and User Guide on 11/1/10

MIND

Mind – i'll start here by saying that your mind is not your brain, well it is and it isn't. Let's go on, your brain is truly amazing, the most powerful transmitter / transponder, receiver, computer on the planet. We transmit and receive vibration as thought. An example of this is ESP, when we think about someone and then they ring or message you, and you say, "oh what a coincidence" , or you ring them and they say, funny, i was just thinking about you, ……yes you were, you were putting out vibration, thought, which the other person picked up on, received, hence…transponder. There's more to this as the rabbit warren goes deeper but i haven't put it in this book, as there hasn't been much of a lead up to allow you to understand just how in tune and powerful we can be, and how connected we are to the rest of the universe, again CWG covers quite a bit of this.

So back to the brain for a bit, ...it's made of cells, as everything is, that are intelligent, hence the intelligent cells in your brain being part of your mind. It has a bunch of tubes that send electrical signals to all parts of our body to move and work and pump our organs and feel and see and hear and smell etc, and it receives and transmits signals via vibration, thought, both consciously and unconsciously. It is also a hard drive for memory, and operates like a computer, programmed by you (as spirit) and everyone else who you have ever been in contact with or heard or seen, ...it holds every memory from when initially conceived (and more) into physical form but has unremembered everything known from non-physical source energy you (spirit). Why have you done that prior to arrival…… so you can experience everything Earth has to offer, nothing more nothing less, as previously mentioned, it's just up to you how you experience this trip, a quick journey to Earth, ...you can take it by the horns and go nuts or sit in the pub and drink beer, your choice, either way it's an experience, just the latter probably won't lead you out of the jungle to your YBR. So coming here is just some fun, where else can you experience ocean, sand, cold, hot, love, laughter, sadness, despair, anxiety, depression, orgasms, riding a bike, climbing a tree, first kiss, flying a plane, and so on, it's a pretty cool planet. I know a lot of you will question all this but that's actually good, because through that thinking and asking yourself questions or reading other books to find your answers, you are nurturing my seed, which will continue to lead you out of the jungle, and that's my goal.

So back to mind, it's the collective of all your

intelligent cells in your body, along with your soul, your spirit and all your memories, beliefs, opinions and ego, all mixed into one happy place. Your filters are running constantly, feeding you all kinds of crap, which makes for soul and spirit to be unclear at times, as well as your choices.   It's all the voices, …..spirit, soul, & ego, …coming through your filters. If you're not aware of your ego, or soul voice, or what crap your memory bank is full of, and all you hear are a bunch of voices saying yes or no along with mixed feelings, ….then it's pretty hard to determine if what you are thinking is true, or right, or wise, or beneficial, or loving, or financially smart, …..or just something you are making up…a story…..which is the case most of the time…i'm fat, i'm ugly, i'm sure he thinks i'm stupid…..am i…?…..bla bla bla…..lol. It really is hard work isn't it, it's constant, ….but the good news is that you can change these thought patterns, and define who's who by re-programming your subconscious….your filters,

..........to be covered soon.

EGO

Ego – can be seen as satan, the devil, sin, evil temptations, and so on, ...but to me it's your negative perception about you and everything else, created by those crappy ideas that are imbedded deep into our subconscious, and a good indication that they're negative is that you're still in the jungle, which is the majority of the people on this planet. Our filters have pathed the way you think and make choices, so if you're racist, that opinion has most likely come from an event that happened at some point in your life and been imbedded into your subconscious, and now you live through that thought your whole life unless you consciously scratch that record, or delete that file. If you believe that all men are ass holes, which was created from some type of trauma or a past incident that created an anchor in your memory to the extent that it went straight to the pool room, your subconscious, and sits there like a dusty old trophy but stands out every time you see, talk, meet, or think about a male, so it ain't doin you any favours for a relationship, or at work with your associates or supervisor or boss, or socially, or at the night club, ……..and until you scratch that record or delete that file, it'll cause you grief. Tony Robbins calls these moments in life 'Anchor Points', it's those opinions and beliefs we hold about ourselves and others, that we revert our thinking to every time we make a decision or perception. It will cause you to doubt most of your ideas or thinking around a certain subject, even the small ones like throwing a coin in the busker's hat, you think you should throw a coin but that thought (ego) will say, don't, you need the money more or he probably makes more than you, or he should go get a real job, or shit he's a male stuff him, or some rubbish like that. To beat ego and kick it in the ass, throw that god damn coin in, in fact, throw a note in and tell the busker, "Well done...love ya stuff...!" and feel you've just bought them a beer or a meal, feel good about it, hell even tell others you did it, be proud and drive your ego home, so when you approach another busker you won't hear from ego, you won't think twice about donating. Yes i know, this could get expensive so just start walking down streets without buskers ......lol.

There's more to it than that, you really need a coach to revisit these original incidents or moments in your life that created your anchor points and relive them and the feelings you had around them and then visualize the person creating that crappy thought or belief is wearing a clown suit, or apologising to you or seeing it as their mistake, replacing the crap memory with a funny or positive one

.....there are various ways of scratching this recorded memory but i'm not gonna track further with this in this book, i suggest you take on a coach to help, like i did.

You have to learn to beat ego up, to a point it just gives up on that subject, knowing you'll win but it will stick it's ugly head up on the next subject, and you need to do the same, until there comes a time it will occur less and less as you become clearer on your path, following your YBR, ...from then on it will only come up on some old crap you haven't yet got rid of or had forgotten about, coming up due to an experience of some sort, again coaches are great to dig this stuff up and get rid of it once and for all. My coach Holly has had to belt me around the ears from time to time but i gave her permission to do that and we're getting there, she has made me trust in soul, listen to soul, confirming soul's presence, i should have done it years ago. I always told myself that i can't really afford a good coach but now i know i can't afford not to have one, and the universe makes those funds available if you just let go and have faith. If you think you haven't got issues preventing you moving forward but you're not where you want to be or living the life that feels right, then you're only kidding yourself, ...they may just be minor or they may be major and effecting you finding your true path here on Earth, it's really hard for you to admit it, as your ego is playing you all the time, telling you that you don't need a coach, you'll sort your own shit out, and so on, again you have the free will to choose.

Just know, before becoming aware of all this stuff, ego can be very dangerous, an example is Hitler, he perceived that to achieve his passion to save humanity and create a pure race he needed to wipe out those that were unconforming including the Jewish culture, and he held legendary status by his subordinates. Humans commit suicide due to their perception of life on Earth being worthless or too hard, just by listening to the wrong voice, which leads on to what they attract, as Hitler did, more about this later.

Ego can be said to stand for 'edging God out', in other words, edging soul out, silencing soul's voice, your only true gift and guide to a great life here on Earth, no wonder some call it satan or the devil, ……..it has fucked with your life all your life. It has silenced your only connection to spirit, your true non-physical source. Sorry about the language but that's the only word shocking enough in the english vocabulary to bring that point home, ………every crap or weak decision you made or didn't make is due to ego, it can destroy you, it can send you into a spiral to hell on Earth, such as suicide, it is the cause of most suicides when at it's extreme. It will say every bad thing to stir you up and make you feel like shit, it will deliberately make you decline good decisions, or not find that right partner, or not stay healthy, or not lose that weight, or not earn that money, or not go on that holiday, ...it's a prick...... learn to recognize it and control it. In the next chapter i will explain how to scratch that record of ego, delete your crap files, your old programming, run an anti-virus and reload with new software. This needs to be done to hear and align with soul clearly, to be confident of its directions to your YBR.

To finish this chapter i wish to point out that your strengths and accomplishments are brought about through the opposite to ego, the good thoughts about yourself, that you are confident about and believe to be true about yourself, (ie) you have great co-ordination, you are good looking, you are quite literate, you have neat handwriting, you always smell nice, you are strong, your hair is gorgeous, your eyes are gorgeous, you are quite athletic, ……..all those things people have reminded you about as you grew up, those moments when people made you feel good about yourself, …..they all go to the pool room as well, and continue to play their part through your filtered thoughts throughout your life. We want to learn to tap into them more regularly and add to them.

The people you know who have a bright outlook on life or generally successful and have been most of their lives may come from a background of positive upbringing, not necessarily wealthy, just a great outlook on life. Those that are leading happy or content lives have naturally learned to contain ego, to scratch their doubting record, delete the viruses and replace with positive software, they read, learn, and listen to uplift and program themselves to follow good feeling thoughts, without knowing where these thoughts are from. It's like some people are just naturally athletic or strong or smart or have a great memory or naturally driven, and some of us have to work for it, re-configure our programming, delete the viruses and work on the system but eventually we have a clean running program, that's clear and easy to follow, that works perfectly and continually updates to become more and more efficient. It's endless the realities of what seeds i'm putting out here, you'll see, ….as mentioned earlier, it's a Pandora's box to the universe, infinity lessons to learn, all waiting for you to accept by listening and trusting soul. There are so many things at play here it isn't black and white but i think you understand now what impression or impact our upbringing and programmed thoughts can have on us as we grow up, especially as a child, so be very careful what you're saying, even out of frustration or anger, and even if it's not your child, you don't know how they look up to you. Be aware of what they may take on from your beliefs and opinions, your outburst or constant inspiration. Be aware of why you make the decisions you make, say the things you say, what life events has this come from, again a coach is a great way to uncover what is going on in the pool room.

SOUL

Soul – as discussed earlier is not a single entity, it's a place or part of you from which to listen to your intuition which are your guides speaking to you, the collective, some call them Sirians, Pleiadians, Lyrans and Arcturians. Some have money guides, happiness guides, purpose guides, love guides, and so on, but all connected to God and the real YOU, non-physical you, helping you re-member who you really are, re-minding you why you came here and **how to stay on your YBR**, …..to me the most important reason to listen to intuition (soul). Yes we're here for fun and experience but again, that's through living out our true purpose while here, not just living un-aware.

A fitting quote from Abraham:

"Physical human has found many labels that they use, depending on how they feel in the moment, to try to describe their interaction with Nonphysical. We are Source Energy. We are Collective Consciousness – meaning a stream. We are a consensus of many (what you might call) Nonphysical voices. We are that which some have called angel. We are that which some have called God. We are that which some have called Inner Being. But most importantly (and we'll use some of our favorite words again) we are focalized Consciousness, specifically responding to the vibration that you manage in your asking."

Excerpted from Portland, OR on 7/12/03 Our Love Esther (Abraham and Jerry)

So soul is that quiet voice in the background that continually tells me to; pick up that tool, not buy those smokes, take a left turn instead of right, stay in bed rather than go to work today, switch off the tv, turn on the radio at a particular time, write a book, go have some fun, ……..and i'm still learning to trust it and to take action on those thoughts but the more i do the more life is evolving towards my true path, and it's becoming exciting ……thanx soul, ……but remember you need to be quiet and still to hear at times.

It's your turn to be here on Earth and play out your game of life on Earth, it's your tour but at the same time making it a better place while you're here. Our guides have all been here before but now they've returned to non-physical source energy, they guide us in making our experience a great one, of love, peace, fulfillment and purpose. Our indigenous from around the world have practiced to listen and learn from those that have passed through, and are now guiding them.

How many times do you regret not grabbing

that tool from the ute and having to walk all the way back cursing you didn't listen to your intuition, me heaps ....lol. The times you just wanted to tell someone to fuck off but that's just not you, you're non confrontational and you don't swear, ...but maybe you would've learned something about yourself and courage or taught that other person something about respect, which helps both of you on your journey. How about the times you've walked past the busker without donating and for the next 10 minutes you kick yourself that you didn't throw in a coin, saying "damn they were good too, damn i'm a tight ass....!" .....or not telling someone that they're awesome or you love them or tell them they're a great mate as this stuff's soft and outside the 'man barrier', and then you kick yourself later, especially if something happens to that person and you don't get to tell them, because that's all they needed to hear to get to the next day. This is so important with family, tell your kids and your wife you love them every day, say goodbye in the morning and wish them an awesome day, because every time you talk yourself out of doing this stuff, ...boom, ...ego right there, ...learn to recognize it, it'll suck you in. Be strong, don't care what other people think, be grateful and proud, tell people they're awesome .....it makes their day, and hell we all can do with that. But in short, follow those quiet voices inside, that gut feeling, to say or do something, just do it and you'll see it'll turn out good.

Before i go further into soul i want to just talk about heaven and hell, ...again for the critics, these are my beliefs, not facts or gospel, ...heaven on Earth is that good feeling when you're excited, happy, ecstatic, in love, having an orgasm, all of the above, on a role, loving your journey, basking on the beach in paradise, having no worries or concerns in this world, damn even the feeling after a couple glasses of wine if that's what it takes, ...all the good feeling stuff. Hell on Earth is the opposite to all these, the morning after too much wine, being destitute, suicidal, depressed, having no hope, no dreams, and so on ....these are the people i wish to touch on my journey, it's one of the reasons why i'm writing this book, for it to all make sense and help find their true path. And then there's 'no man's land' ....that place where you're not growing and you're not failing, you're just living day to day in a rut because you're not making any decisions or following your intuition. Sometimes we are like plants if we're not growing we are in fact dying, shriveling up, weeping, requiring nurturing, help, some fertilizer to give us a kick. That's where drugs, alcohol and smoking come into the human existence, for a short term fix, ...or so we think, as everything, they have consequences, no need to go into that again. The fertilizer and nurturing is the best fix,

…..get into some reading, learn to listen to soul, ….so important, it's an immediate fix, and i mean it can be within seconds if you learn to tune in and let go.

So back to soul……..reverting to the jungle is an easy thing to do with so many distractions here on Earth eh…….drugs, greed, power, it's a free world and everything is up for the taking or trying. It's easy for us to be distracted by all that stuff because we have free will, which most other animals don't have, (ie) we're not pre-programmed to eat grass, breed and moo. Free will can work to our benefit and detriment, ….you can wander off the path as many times as you like due to free will distractions or you can make decisions in your life through free will like leaving a job, your partner, your town or country, or a change in gender, the world is your oyster, there are no boundaries, only the boundaries you put on yourself, the limits you put on your courage, listen to where your soul wants to take you. It may be taking on a business or adventure or writing a poem, wearing your hair differently or changing what you wear, ...they're generally the fun, exciting, adventurous, scary callings, that take courage to fulfill but they will lead you on to your YBR, it is your GPS for your journey, it will keep recalculating every time you take a wrong turn or once you've succeeded a goal, but if you're not moving at all you may end up in 'no man's land', but soul is still with you then, sending you signals, ...you need to be looking for heaven on Earth, and wanting to leave hell on Earth, you need to ask and soul will deliver, it will give you directions to follow, like clockwork, constantly, as long as you are tuned in, ...as long as you are consciously listening, and at times this will even be while induced with alcohol or drugs, believe it or not. Have a think about some of the greatest musical albums ever made, some of the greatest pieces of art ever painted or drawn, how a lot of the indigenous people visit other planes for an answer, using an induced state purely to remove inhibitions. Make your own mind up about that, again these are my own beliefs that i'm simply writing out, and certainly not advising to go get smashed to visit heaven…..lol.

Once you learn to follow your intuition, listen to soul and live by its guide it will naturally become clearer. What makes the message unclear is ego, …..it's filters blur and confuse the messages, …..it creates doubt, but tell it you're in control, not gonna get sucked in anymore, …..go with the **feel good** messages, trust them, learn to listen to soul, the quiet voice and see the changes in your life, bit by bit.

SPIRIT

Spirit – for me, i am spirit and within me as my non-physical source energy i have a body, my human existence....the bag of bones made up of cells etc, ...like your aura if you like but much bigger, as it is interconnected throughout the universe to anything and everything......it is "I AM".....yes i know.....a bit much.....but do your own research. When you depart this planet and become fully aware again, back to being non-physical, dumping your bag of bones and handing your cells back to the planet, in human terminology 'dying'....you don't actually die, you simply return to your non- physical awareness self as source energy, and you'll still have this awareness of you, you've always had it, always will have it, in the hundreds of visits prior and if you decide to visit again, …….yes i believe in reincarnation. Have you ever wondered why you have an attraction to flying, or sailing, or royalty, or art or notice how some kids are attuned to music or musical instruments almost before they can walk, how they take to science or architecture or language at a young age. Do you ever wonder if you've been somewhere before but just can't put your finger on it, and the examples are endless. Have your own thoughts about this, do your own research on it but i know what feels right to me, again i refer back to the CWG trilogy or look up Esther Hicks (Abraham), …..it's pretty cool stuff, not everyone is barking up the wrong tree or making all this up just to fool y'all….lol.

Sooo, …as a spirit i am connected to God, and here's the kicker, i am God, ….i can hear a lot of readers now, …..you what, you think you're

God, ……lol, …..we all are. If God is everything, all, the universe, energy, and spirit, and spirit is us, our non-physical self, then yes we are part of God but as humans on Earth we are like God's fingertips. God, non-physical us, experiences through us as physical us, experiencing love, hate, fear, excitement and so on. There is nothing that God has not seen or heard, so that's why there is no right or wrong, ….what is swearing, alcohol, blasphemy, murder, passion, ecstasy, and so on …….simply Earthly experiences that we as humans experience, and God (us in non-physical form) experiences also, …….it's only our human perceptions through culture and upbringings and teachings that cause us to decide how we feel about subjects on Earth, a lot of this culture coming from many edited versions of the Bible, which again is a great read but for me personally i find different religions taking different takes on the scriptures, so who do you believe, …..i believe my heart, how it makes me feel when i read it, i believe in what my gut says, …….who knows, i may read it again in years to come and get a whole new understanding or ah ha moment when i've progressed in my spiritual journey, knowing more, and i might not but i'm open to it all. In fact i love the JW's or Seventh Dayer's coming around for a chat with them over a cuppa, to get their views on life, or God, or who we are, why we're here, …….the best question is about the dinosaurs, …..i get a lot of different answers with that one …..lol …..and just to confirm, i'm not ridiculing them, i just like to have some fun, and at times they look at me and probably think…."cuckoo"….lol. But in all seriousness they're nice folk and believe what they believe and i love them equally, from one soul to another, they're on their own journey, the same as everyone else and we never stop learning.

Some of this can be difficult to swallow if you

have followed a religion for some time or never, but all i ask is you have an open mind, don't sign off from what your ego is saying, listen to your heart, does it sound intriguing or possible, if so, then maybe do some further research, look into CWG or other teachers that take your fancy. I have no financial affiliation with CWG by the way, in case some of you are thinking that, it simply changed the way i think and feel and literally helped me find my way out of my jungle. Funny, my mum threw the book down in disgrace when i first showed her, "blasphemy" she said, ……and now she lives and breathes Neale Donald Walsch, not bad coming from a lady that spent most of her life in an Apostolic Church, even preaching on the streets, ……..so yes, i know a bit about religion and theology, and find some of it fascinating, with great ideals to live by, and certainly comfort in some churches and their groups but with others way too extreme for me, and this isn't the time to write about all that. God is part of all the churches and those that follow them, and as much a part of the Masonic Lodge, and every other group and cult and society out there, God is all and experiencing Earth through us, the spirit has created our physical body to feel those experiences.

You as your spirit is your non-physical awareness, that knows all but has chosen to forget each time coming here so that you can re-learn, …un-forget, …un-become a human and have some fun while learning and adding to the growth of this planet, you become aware, if you choose. You're actually doing this in other places also at the same time but that's for another time also or your own further research. There's nothing more, nothing less to do here, it's pretty simple yeah, it's just that human's are taking a bit to get it. Our mates out there, …….souls, guides, the collective, send us a helping hand every now and then to give us a kick up the ass, ……. Jesus, Buda, Galileo, Einstein, Gandhi, Esther Hicks, Neale Donald Walsch and many others, ……known as masters, ……and even after these hand outs a lot of us still refuse to believe, and revert back to the jungle and think we know better, or listen to ego. As a collective race we could have made better choices, with different thinking we could produce better outcomes with less detrimental consequences to our planet and its people, …..choices around mother nature, improving humanity and the planet. Wouldn't it be great to see the worlds societies become focused on collective goals. I really believe that one day people in power will run our countries for love of their country and not for profit or financial reward……i wonder how many would do it for free, …..mmm maybe Donald Trump, ……damn that'll stir the pot. Imagine the wealthy willfully taking up the slack in taxes to help out those less in tune, removing the large burden on lower and middle class, paying a larger percentage with regard to their incomes. Helping those on unemployment benefits or those living on the street to find their cause, …..we've just grown a culture to think that everyone should go to school or work, regardless if that's our passion or not, rather than follow what feels right, ….the hard ass's say, "get off your ass, go to school or get a job, earn a dollar, do something for your country", ……and i say that's all crap. Why not allow our youth to follow their passions, …..as Einstein said,

"Everybody is a genius, but if you judge a fish by its ability to climb a tree, it will live its whole life believing that it is stupid."

Let our youth follow what they love doing, and educate them using passionate mentors, not always books. We need to stop force feeding our youth with crap they don't need or will use, they'll find that stuff through growing up and living, then deciding which direction they'll choose, ……which may involve education or trades or a job, as everyone has different likes but it also may involve receiving benefits so they can spend time helping the needy, creating music or art or following a dream, or designing architecture, or saving the whales or trees, it may be teaching those caught in the lower socioeconomic jungle in how to take hold of their lives. I know our economy would get a bit of a shake up but it would soon work out. Imagine the suffering some of our street people endure, yes they're human beings, with souls and spirit, temporarily lost, unaware, lonely, freezing at night, concrete beds, no money, no food, no water, no happiness, just lost in the jungle……our prisoners are better looked after, it's bullshit. I've experienced having no income or money, i've been on benefits, used govt handouts, …….and i'm telling you for me back then it was the worst feeling, my pride was gone from not fitting in, failing as the bread winner, i felt quite lost as a man. The term 'dole bludger' is certainly a derogatory and idealistic generalizing label that's typically been created by ozzies, ……..we tend to do that, ……..most of the time more in a humorous way, though often our sayings or labels get used out of context. Some of those on 'the dole' don't want to work because they want to 'save the planet' or are 'tree huggers' or are 'greenies' but imagine if we didn't have these people that are connected to mother earth, fighting for a cause, having the courage to stand up to the rest of us and stop us stripping the rain forests, damming natural waterways, saving whales from extinction due to greed, and so on. We seem to forget or filter out the frustrations these people must have with the average "she'll be right mate!" person, who really doesn't go out of their way at all to play a part in the betterment of humanity, except for throwing a can or stubby in the recycle bin, donating to the occasional charity. Again, this is not everyone, because i can hear some of you now, "so what have you done to save the planet, what makes you so right?" Nothing out of the ordinary, i'm one of the people i'm talking about, if that makes sense. I'm merely making a point that we can change our culture to become more open minded, accept those that we believe don't fit in to societies mold, let's start thinking about giving our kids a say.....as they come fresh from spirit, ...they haven't been corrupted too much by old school teachings yet..... they speak truth and are transparent, lets listen to their ideas. There's no right or wrong, just choices and with choices come consequences, if we screw up so be it, we try again but surely we could learn from all our screw ups, ...can't someone write a book covering off all humanities historic screw ups, then Part II could be

'Living life on Earth without screw ups' as an instructional guide......yeah i can hear the religious now....it's called a Bible you idiot!......lol. I believe that one seed at a time we will slowly evolve into a humane and understanding race, that loves, feels, and understands purpose for any individual, regardless or their education or background. I see a transparent world government, unlike our current UN or elite groups like the Bilderberg Group or the Rothmans or so on, taking on and implementing ideas that are voted by all the people, yes it's a distance away and i probably won't see it in my life time but it will give hope, confidence and trust back to humanity, reducing unnecessary war and poverty, there will always be the rebels but they'll become less over time. I see a vast improvement or advances on self education, medicines, fuels, inventions, finances, taxes, and the list goes on. It sounds too good to be true but bit by bit it will happen as people evolve and grow into alignment with who they are. There are a lot of masters here on Earth who can guide the true values and ideas for the human race to advance towards alignment, and they will continue to come. As corny as it sounds, our si-fi movies have some incredible inventions and ideas, most that will come about in time but the ideas for these have been passed along from soul, again to give us a hint here and there. So as we all learn to listen, becoming aware, and bit by bit move into alignment, imagine the changes that will come, the ideas that will flow but it has to infiltrate the ones that currently make our decisions, and it will, in time. As people become aware so the changes will be made, it's inevitable. So for those wondering about our future due to our current position, i believe it's a fruitful one, an exciting one, one that will bring health back to the people, less stressful, more fun, it'll be like taking on a new job that we're excited about, that we want to work at but it won't be work because we'll be doing it for love, money as we know it won't be around. It won't be about greed or balanced off gold, it'll be about our contribution to humanity and the planet, our food and housing and expenses will be covered like credits for contribution. There's way more to this and i reckon it'll end up as a book one day, if soul so wishes......lol. Some countries like Finland are already heading this way, with education and systems like the UBI for the unemployed to focus on their passions. These concepts will continue to spread world wide, ...a great bloke (in my opinion) or series to watch is Corey Whites Roadmap to Paradise, he makes some great points as a comedian.

Crap, that was a bit heavy, ...anyway back to spirit, ...we do things in the spirit of fun, in the spirit of love, it's terminology is used to name an emotion, as it is how we feel at the time, and when we feel love, that is the pinnacle of spirit. Love is a great feeling, things go well when we are in love, you attract the right people and circumstance when you show love. It's not always easy to stay in this frame of mind if you're not doing what you love, or not following a passion that you love, because you are being told or made to do something you don't love, like work a crap job to make the world go round. Just a thought, make your own mind up about this.

CONSCIOUS & SUBCONSCIOUS

How do i control or change my filters? How do i scratch my record, where do i get the anti-virus to delete the unwanted crap and then download the new software to re-program my system and way of thinking? What are my conscious thoughts? What are my subconscious thoughts? Well read on………

You can read books and attend courses like Anthony Robins or 'Landmark' which are pretty cool, …..hell you can even Google it, but i'll get you started.

When talking to yourself, whether through Spirit or Soul or Ego, these voices otherwise known as thought are coming from your mind, as previously discussed. You as spirit and soul and ego all think through your conscious mind while you're awake, while conscious of actually thinking but due to being awake or conscious you can filter these thoughts and immediately decide what you perceive to be right or wrong, fact or fiction, and respond in a way that is the result of putting together everything you think you know or believe and making a decision or response, not always soul's suggestion or to your benefit, because you don't know what's right or wrong, it's all merely a perception or opinion from what you think you know. The only true path to happiness and love and peace is by consciously listening to soul and actioning its suggestion. It is always the best option but you must learn to hear and trust and follow soul when in a conscious state, ignoring ego and other opinions.

Your subconscious is full of your life's program, playing out on auto pilot like a record player or a computer program in the background, influencing everything you do and think without you even know it's going on, whether awake or asleep or in a meditative trance, it's your physical makeup imbedded into your memory bank from every memory since physical conception of you as a human. I once heard Wayne Dyer say that we operate about 97% of our time from our subconscious mind, so what if what's in there isn't real good, i mean.....negative, are you then asking to attract negative things into your life about 97% of the time, ...damn ......that's scary! ....sad face.

Your subconscious started out clean and full of love from mum but as time goes on it gets polluted with every experience and feeling experienced via your conscious mind. It begins to create a picture of who you are and that changes as you experience more but a lot of the strong experiences like trauma, or excitement stay buried as anchor points for your now becoming personality, and so it goes. Depending on what is going in creates what is showing out. Imagine how complex this must be for every decision or thought you make for a middle aged human, crazy feat of engineering but can lead you up the garden path to ruin or riches.

The great thing is that all these memories or programs can be scrubbed or changed and deleted. See, you think about some of these moments in your life as horrible or exciting or scary or frustrating or degrading or uplifting but again, it is all perception at the time you experienced them. If your mum or dad said out of anger one day while young, "why can't you be like your brother/sister" you most likely took that as a life changing criticism and live in to it today, and always have thoughts that your brother/sister is the preferred or favourite and you'll never be as good, ……imagine what that could do to a child then adolescent and into adulthood, …..massive confidence killer right there, creating a ripple effect throughout their life effecting career, family, relationships, and so on. It sounds trivial but these events repeated all through your life can be fatal, literally, and if not fatal can cause some long term suffering and anguish that they're not loved, like their parents just threw them away. I think you're getting the picture and can possibly relate from experience.

So, these thoughts are generally forgotten, as they're down in the pool room never looked at, dusty, just sitting there until needed, ……when are they needed, when a decision is to be made involving this memory, which is often. You live into these memories through your filters daily, not realising they're still down in the pool room. One way to change them out for new is to go to the pool room, pick up that trophy, re-visit the experience of getting that trophy.....yes tears and anger and yelling and all if needed, and then forgive the one that made the comment, whether your parents, the bully at school, your brother or sister, your teacher, whoever, just picture them standing in front of you saying that they're absolute dickheads for saying that but you realise they meant nothing by it, in fact they're even wearing a clown outfit, or joking with you saying, damn i thought you found it funny, i so didn't mean to hurt you, and so on. You shake their hand, tell them you love them and walk away, a bigger person, strong, happy you've sorted that shit out once and for all. There are many ways to do this, and i'm certainly no expert, so please seek advice from a coach or the likes of 'Landmark' or Anthony Robbins, or whoever you choose to help this process but do something, and begin the process of re-programming your subconscious with thoughts and knowledge of peace, love, happiness, excitement, courage and the like, so that you live into these things daily without thinking and watch the change in your life with little or no effort, and how much more clear soul becomes.

Depending on how many trophies there are to find, layers or years to peel back, is how long this process will take but eventually you'll scratch all the record of doubt and crap, and replace it with a new record that you will love listening to constantly, and never get sick of. I took on Holly as a coach, as i struggled to scratch my record on my own, EGO had a good hold and i couldn't afford a good coach but more importantly i couldn't afford not to have one. I've read, listened and learned a lot of stuff over 10+ years, some call it personal development but a lot of it is crap and confusing if you don't understand how to apply it. There were seeds of info in it all but until i started chatting with Holly nothing changed, i became frustrated, ego was going all out on me, especially because i thought i knew better, and i still couldn't work it out. As soon as i started with coaching in a matter of weeks i started seeing changes, became more in tune with my true purpose and started following it. I learned how to recognize ego and stomp on its head. There's still a lot of old dusty trophy's hiding down there but Holly and i will find them and smash em, and already the pool room is looking fresher, cleaner, with new pictures of positive sayings on the walls and some new trophy's that shine and that i'm proud of. Holly has been instrumental in my journey, and helped me clear enough space to start renovating for new trophy's through following her guidance and soul, being one of the same. So as your journey unfolds or you unbecome as your physical self, be very conscious of what you're thinking, willfully think only about what you want, who you want to be, where you want to be, this will attract more of the things you want but think and visualise that you are already there or have these things to get rid of the wanting component, and start all your affirmations or requests with "I AM". The majority of thoughts have to be positive to start changing your path from the jungle to your YBR. Your life will continue to evolve and grow through this.

I hope this all made some sense, ……..so now the question…….how do we keep attracting crap into our lives, besides from our ego or filters…..how does it come from what we think…….is it just our actions and decisions we make…….? Read on……..

LAW OF ATTRACTION

Law of Attraction – Funny, i remember when i was first writing this book i saw a saying on a calendar at my old workplace *"Welcome to the jungle"*, i thought that was funny, just a reminder that working a job to pay bills is the jungle, and i'm still there even though i do work for myself....lol.

Most of you are familiar with Law of Attraction but if you're not, here's an overview. It's our gift from God or the universe, whatever you believe, ……."ask and you shall receive" or "you are what you think" or "as we think we are"…..and so on. It can be a curse to those in the jungle or a gift to those who master it, either way it gives you what you ask for, what you're thinking, without prejudice, so be aware that it's there.

I mentioned in a previous chapter that as we think we transmit those thoughts as vibration, energy, picked up by other people anywhere on the planet, or universe for that matter. These thoughts, vibrations, energy, create and attract a like thought into who ever or what ever is in tune, throughout the universe. As these thoughts align with similar energy they begin to manifest into physical form by manipulating the collective consciousness (society) to make whatever you're asking to happen, without us even knowing.

Similar to a previous example, ……you think of Jill for whatever reason and then Jill receives those thoughts and Jill says to herself, ..."i think i'll call Jack", and low n behold you get a call, ...some would say by pure coincidence but i believe otherwise. In a physical example think of 2 drops of water touching each other, their molecules and energies create that attraction and they join. It's no different to our thoughts as energy transmitting out and about, throughout the universe.

Another example is that you think continually that you never have enough income or money to get on top of your bills, and guess what, you don't, again not a coincidence. This goes on for relationships, health, finances, absolutely everything. It's not instantaneous though, luckily the thoughts are to be for at least 17 seconds to start the connection. Imagine if they were instantaneous, we'd be in all sorts of shit.

Once the like vs like, the molding of the parts, the law of attraction starts, it will begin to create your wishes, good or bad, yes that's right good or bad. This human gift is designed to help us bring peace, love, health and abundance into our lives but we need the right subconscious programming to naturally think like that on auto pilot as that's the place the majority of our thinking come from, even when awake. When conscious it can be easier if you have the will power to focus regularly on your desires, but it can be also quite difficult to imagine a life of peace and harmony if you're broke, in debt, sleeping on the streets, in jail, on drugs, in a crap relationship, have an illness or dis-ease, or life is just treating you like crap. Dis-ease is a big one in my opinion with Law of Attraction, it's all around us, more and more people suffer from dis-ease or illnesses, driven by depression, anxiety, hatred, ….imagine what's going through their thoughts every day, people are attracting dis- ease like cancers through L of A. I've seen people who hated what they saw in the mirror and actually got cancer on their face which had to be cut out leaving scarring and a resemblance of what they initially saw. I could discuss this item for pages, but i think you see where i'm going, and it'll get a few people on their back foot if i go further. Again, make your own mind up and do some research, incl how to cure dis-ease using L of A, works the same way.

Some are saying, "what about babies or kids....?" and that's for another conversation, but try Esther Hicks (Abraham) for starters.

An interesting excerpt from Abraham:

"Babies Are Thinking and Attracting Before They Are Speaking... Even though you are only months old in your physical body, you are a very old and wise creator focused in that baby's body. And you came

with powerful intentions to experience contrast and to launch clear rockets of desire into your Vibrational Reality for the purpose of expansion. People often assume that because a child is not yet offering words, the child could not be the creator of its own experience but it is our promise to you that no one else is creating your experience. Children emanate Vibrations which are the reason for what they attract - even from their time of birth."

Excerpted from The Vortex on 8/31/09 Esther (Abraham and Jerry)

Another example are healings in a church, full of people thinking powerfully about the same thing. Imagine the energy being emitted while focusing on one thing for quite a period of time to cure that guy/gal down the front. Some say it's a farce, or bs, ...believe what feels right, ...to me it just makes sense that all that focus will definitely have an effect, especially with such belief and love and feeling from both the congregation and individual with the ailment.

It doesn't have to be in a church, there's plenty of evidence of groups of people, good or bad, wanting the same thing bad enough, believing in it, visualizing life with it in place, and low and behold, it happens, whether over time or immediately depends on the conviction. Every invention can prove that, every charity organisation, every war, every feat of courage, everything starts off as a thought, and through L of A it's manifested through manipulation of all the moving parts into the outcome.

We do have will-power though, that's the power of free will or choice, in other words we can attract in to our life whatever with think on a regular basis, our most constant thoughts, so if you're in a shitty situation you can change that in 2 ways, ………start listening to soul, and start visualizing yourself where you want to be. Visualise and feel these dreams as being there now, you must do this to attract it. The more you do it, feel it, imagine it, visualize it, regardless of your current situation, the more you will start to see changes, taking you towards those goals, but if you fall off the path back into the jungle and lose sight of your YBR you will start attracting whatever is on auto pilot (subconscious) again, it can take a while to attract what you want, and for some they attract it quicker than others, it's about focus and belief.

Yes i know, it's Pandora's Box yeah, …..i can hear you saying, "how hard is it to keep this up, to stay focused", …….bloody hard…! It takes courage and will power to remain focused on the right things, … constantly listening out for soul, and it's signs, ….going to sleep at night with good feeling thoughts of your dreams and goals, picture them and fall asleep imagining you living them out, ……..it all works together to break your crappy habits and mindset, your auto pilot subconscious. Your mind, your thoughts, don't know reality from fiction when thinking, your senses tell you what you're feeling……sadness, guilt, happiness etc, and that's what you attract, what you're feeling but when you consciously visualize a goal or dream or feeling, it also believes that is real and happening and sends you more of it but because when we're in the jungle most of our conscious thoughts are crap and that's what we continually attract to our lives, which keeps us in the jungle, so stay tuned on what you're thinking most of the time, have the courage and determination and will power to keep it up. Listen out for soul at the same time and bit by bit you'll get there, back on your path to take on the next chapter but remember, it gets easier and easier as you build these skills and habits, as you change the way you think, ………use the Law of Attraction to your advantage. A fun one to try is visualizing a vacant car park right near the entry to the shopping centre, see it, feel the excitement of it being there, and you watch, 9 times out of 10 it'll either be there or it'll appear as a car just pulls out as you're pulling up. As a family we always do this, we take it in turns to try but remember you want to be going for about 17+ seconds to make it work. You can use this in a heap of other ways, just start and practice.

I wasn't sure where to put this paragraph but felt it important to write, …….every time you think of someone, they will think of you, whether they respond is their choice but here's the doozy, and sorry if you're of indigenous culture, …….but every time you think of someone who has passed away, back to non-physical, they are with you immediately in spirit form, some people will even say that they could feel their presence, i'll leave it there but remember what i wrote in Ch 2 & 7 about spirit, it is you, always will be, always was, it is your God form, ...that's bound to stir the pot with a few......lol. Again, my beliefs don't have to be yours, do your own research or just go with what feels right and feels good, that'll be the right answer. With ESP, as we develop as a race we'll become more in tune to use this, some people already can.

To summarise, find a coach, clean out that pool room and replace with good feeling thoughts, then allow Law of Attraction to do it's job with your new found thinking and feeling both consciously and through subconscious, ...it's the physical gift you have here on Earth, start listening to Soul and believe in those thoughts, those good feeling voices, follow them, and watch your life change, and as it changes for the better it will compound to become outright exciting, and ego will be silenced through your love for life, ego will starve, it can't thrive on love.

LET GO
&
LET BE

The art of letting go is just that, throwing your hands in the air, dropping the rains, handing over management to your soul, it's learning to control thought, letting go takes practice, it works when you believe soul is looking after you, …….have faith. Until you believe this you can't let go, so what is letting go….? Taking a deep breath, relaxing all your muscles, especially your stomach muscles, and just knowing it'll turn out ok, and it's funny, ……as soon as you do that under all circumstances it feels like the world of burdens have lifted off your shoulders, and then you'll see the magic happen, ...is this easy to do, ...in the beginning no definitely not but it gets easier. Ego generally jumps out of its box and tells you that you're idiot, your neglecting your duties as a father, mother, human, staff member, or not being responsible, or not manning up, or being a princess, or you'll simply fail, ...but put ego back in its box, and trust in soul's guidance and outcomes, and that it's actually there with you. Another way is to look at yourself and your huge issues from way out in outer space, seeing planet Earth, and then zooming into that minute important spec of a human somewhere there on the planet, yes that's you in this bigger picture worrying about money, relationships, tattslotto numbers, work, illness, ...and there's a whole universe out there, ...this gives me a perspective on life but eh, it may not work for you ....lol.

If we choose to let go all of the time, ……..let go and let be, ……..we would all be in a better place. The fully aware can't have war, can't allow starving, don't live for greed, work for a passion so it's not work, listen to their young, care for and nurture Earth, don't need to use drugs or medication, eat a healthier diet, don't exist in routine or a rut, and live for the moment. Find out who you really are, what routine or rut you're caught in, what your auto pilot is set to, learn to hear soul and to live by soul and let go more often, then you and me will find our new found life, and along the way plant some seeds and simply start living a happier, more joyful, fulfilling and exciting life knowing there is a reason you are here, ……there is a part you can play, it's waiting for you and has been since you arrived, so grab it, swallow the blue pill, listen intently and start learning to have some fun with the rest of us, telling others who are ready to listen, which won't be everyone, only those that are becoming aware!

So go and spread your wings, listen to your feelings, and attract like minded people to be around, ...life will become an exciting journey, not without challenges but fun, scary at times, adventurous, and it'll have meaning and purpose, ...enjoy.....!

One more from Abraham to finish off............

"It feels so good to realize that the Energy that creates worlds is supporting you; to wake up every morning in clarity, knowing exactly who-you-are; to know that Source is thinking through you; to experience meaningful rendezvous; to dovetail with the right people who give you the right piece of information just at the right time; to never feel dependent upon anyone; to know with clarity who-you-are; to feel the Energy that creates worlds moving through your fingertips and through your mind; to see evidence all around you of the thoughts you have been thinking and to feel the power of who-you-are! That's what you came for."

Excerpted from Phoenix, AZ on 2/1/14 Our Love Esther (Abraham and Jerry)

p.s. If reading this book has left you wondering where to now, go with your soul but you might find yourself in no-man's land for a short period, that's ok.

"Many people who are going through the early stages of the awakening process are no longer certain what their outer purpose is. What drives the world no longer drives them. Seeing the madness of our civilization so clearly, they feel somewhat alienated from the culture around them. Some feel that they inhabit a no-man's-land between two worlds. They are no longer run by the ego, yet the arising awareness has not yet become fully integrated into their lives. Inner and outer purpose have not merged."

Eckhart Tolle

Keep me up to date with your journey, look me

up and send me a line, i'd love to hear your story.

** As i complete this version of True Path, humanity is going through a tough time, ….COVID19. Without going into any of this right now as i could write a whole book on this event and this particular time in humanity, but my suggestion is to follow your heart, your intuition and what feels good. Chat to Soul, listen for advice on how to stay grounded, even in these changing and tumultuous times. Find a coach or some mentors, focus on your good feeling thoughts, focus on thoughts that lead you to a 5D reality, …..thoughts that both Gaia and humanity will conquer as a natural occurrence, ….yes there will be tough times, upheaval, demonstrations, frustration, climatic upheavals, political and royal takedowns, and way more, but in the end those that focus on ascension, 5D, enlightenment and simply trusting that YOU personally will conquer and overcome and move into a place of peace.

Those that get caught up in the darkness, and there's plenty of that, and believe in the 3D illusion will continue to suffer until they choose to alter their state of mind. Remember, it's all perception, ….how you decide to react or think, the Law of Attraction will give you that. It's your choice and no one's fault what you get or where you're at, purely what you attract. Contact me if you struggle with this.

There will be some incredible humanity altering events during all this and in the very near future, and for years to come, some not so good and some good. It will test our rights as humans on this planet and beliefs on where we as a society are heading or ought to head. Are we ready for massive changes, stepping into a whole new way of living. Will we take on a type of NESARA law, reverting back to our lands, our constitutions, transparency, etc. I have no doubt AI will come into our life in a big way, as we've seen in most futuristic movies for years, whether we believe in Bill Gates or Elon Musk or the likes being right or wrong makes no difference, ...how you deal with this personally is the key, ...follow good feeling thoughts and stay tuned in to your guides, physical and non-physical. Life will continue to evolve regardless, it's just how you choose to accept it, react to it, defend it, or simply live with it, ...remember it's all perception. In this 3D illusion that most know as life, everything will always be a struggle due to the low frequency, restricting us. There's a reason for this but maybe that's for another book. Remember it's an illusion, it's only your perception, keep evolving, keep tuning in to your heart, your good feeling thoughts, your guides and it'll turn out to be ok, ...just remember who you are, you are amazing....!!!

Love ya's all, chat soon.....

-- Paul Colquhoun --

REFERENCES

There are plenty of areas from within this book that you may wish to do your own research, but a couple areas to start i've listed below. Information that may clear up a few doubts or questions, or simply take you further in your understanding of what's possible.

Conversations With God
Book trilogy by Neale Donald Walsch

abraham-hicks.com
A daily email and more to keep you on track

louisehay.com
Great for affirmations & self discovery

drwaynedyer.com
Great for understanding TAO & self discovery

gaia.com
Interesting videos and information

tolmanselfcare.com
Don & Tyler Tolman – self care articles

harveker.com
Great for understanding money and spirituality

michaelbernardbeckwith.com
Transforming your life

eckharttolle.com
Experience a life of purpose and presence

Think & Grow Rich
Amazing book by Napoleon Hill

Corey White

Comedian with some great ideas

My email:

followyourtruepath@gmail.com

www.ingramcontent.com/pod-product-compliance
Lightning Source LLC
Chambersburg PA
CBHW032040290426
44110CB00012B/893